# THE Pack IS Back

**PIONEER EDITION**

## By Gary Miller and Paul Tolme

## CONTENTS

# Return *of the* Gray Wolf

WHO'S AFRAID OF THE BIG, BAD WOLF? It used to be everyone!

WOLVES ARE FIERCE HUNTERS. Their teeth can crush bones. No wonder people have always feared them. Today, people understand wolves better. Wolves almost never attack people. Wolves are important to the natural world, too.

Today, the gray wolf has disappeared from most parts of the United States. But people work hard to bring back the wolves. Soon wolf howls may be heard in new places!

## Creatures in Conflict

Gray wolves used to live all across North America. They lived in Mexican deserts. They lived in the cold Arctic.

Sometimes they attacked farm animals. They killed the animals that people hunted for food.

So people began to kill wolves. By 1940, only about 300 survived. Wolves were in trouble.

Wolves are part of the dog family. They live in groups called **packs**. Packs hunt together. Packs share food. Living in packs helps wolves survive.

**Who's the Boss?** *These wolves look dangerous. But they are not really fighting. The wolf on the left shows the other that it is boss. Wolf bosses stand up taller than less powerful wolves.*

## Hoot and Howl

A wolf pack is like a family. There are adults and children. The adult wolves lead the pack.

Wolves use body language to send messages to each other. A wolf pup licks an adult's mouth. This says, "I'm hungry!" The adult spits up food.

Then the pup eats it. Yuck! That may seem disgusting. But to a young wolf, it's a tasty meal.

Wolves also howl to tell each other things. They howl to find each other. They also howl and howl when it's time to hunt.

**Snack Time.** *A wolf pup licks its mother's mouth. This tells her it's hungry.*

**Body Language.** *Wolves touch one another to say hello.*

5

## Pack Attack!

Hunting is important for wolves. An adult gray wolf needs to eat a lot. It needs at least 2.2 kilograms (5 pounds) of meat a day to stay healthy. Wolves hunt large animals that eat plants. Wolves love to eat elk and moose, for example.

Wolves think before they attack. They know hunting can be dangerous. One kick from a moose can kill a wolf. Wolves try to attack the weakest animal. This keeps them safe.

Scientists aren't sure how they do this. Maybe wolves use their eyes. A weak animal may limp. Or a weak animal may move slowly. Or maybe a wolf uses its nose. It may be able to smell sickness in other animals.

**Big Meal.** *Wolves hunt in a pack. Together, they can kill large animals, such as this elk.*

## New Attitudes, New Hope

Have you ever seen a wolf? No? That could change! The wolves are returning in some places. In 1973, people passed a law to protect **endangered** animals. That law helped the wolves. They started to come back.

Some people feel better about wolves now. Few people raise farm animals today. They don't have cows and sheep. They don't worry that wolves will eat their animals.

People also know that wolves help ecosystems. Some animals eat too many plants. Wolves lower the number of these animals. This helps the ecosystem. It keeps it healthy. It keeps it balanced.

## The Wolves Return

There are a lot more wolves now than there were in 1973. Scientists also brought wolves back to Yellowstone National Park in 1995 and 1996.

There are still people who don't want wolves to return. Some ranchers don't. They worry about their farm animals. They worry that wolves will kill their animals.

**Family Ties.** *A wolf pack usually has four to ten family members.*

But wildlife groups have an answer. They pay ranchers for any farm animals killed by wolves.

## Here to Stay

Wolves have come back to areas where they once lived. Today, Minnesota and Wisconsin have them.

Take a walk in the woods if you visit these places. Keep your eyes open. You may see a bit of gray fur. You may hear a howl. If you do, howl back. It's the friendly thing to do.

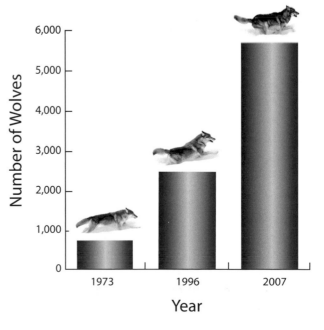

U.S. Gray Wolf Population
(Outside Alaska)

Number of Wolves

6,000

5,000

4,000

3,000

2,000

1,000

0

1973　1996　2007

Year

# THE Pack IS Back

By Paul Tolme

*Wolves are returning in the United States. They help other animals, too.*

DOUG SMITH WAS IN Yellowstone National Park. He watched a wolf **den**, or home. He moved slowly. He was quiet. He did not want to scare the wolves in the den. Soon a wolf came out of the den.

It was a mother wolf. She smelled the air. She looked around for danger. It was safe. Then three wolf pups, or babies, came out of the den.

The pups felt safe. They played in the grass. Smith was glad to see them. The pups showed that more wolves were in the park.

That makes Smith happy. He is a wolf scientist. He studies the gray wolves that live in the park. Lots of wolves used to live here. But these wolves attacked farm animals. So people killed all the wolves.

## Bringing Wolves Back

For 80 years, no wolves lived in Yellowstone. Then Smith brought them back to the park in 1995. This is called **reintroduction**. He did this to keep the habitat of the park healthy.

Wolves help many plants and animals. In Yellowstone, wolves hunt elk. Too many elk used to live in the park. The elk ate all the small plants. Now that the wolves are back, the park has more small plants.

Beavers need small plants for food. Now that there are more small plants, more beavers live in the park, too.

The beavers build dams. This makes ponds. Fish live in the ponds. Eagles eat the fish. Wolves help all these animals by eating the elk.

**Wolf Study.** *Doug Smith checks a wolf. Medicine keeps the wolf still.*

**Growing Numbers.** *This is a gray wolf. It is an endangered species. But the number of gray wolves is growing. They may not be endangered much longer.*

**A Good Nose.** *This red wolf sniffs the ground. Maybe it smells a tasty raccoon.*

## Leftovers

Even elk are helped by wolves. Wolves usually only hunt sick elk. Killing sick animals makes the elk herd stronger.

Other animals are helped, too. They eat the parts of an elk the wolves don't eat. Bears, birds, and foxes eat the leftover elk. That means lots of animals get a free meal.

## The Wolf Effect

Everywhere wolves live there are good changes. These changes are called the "wolf effect."

Smith has seen the wolf effect in the Arctic. That is near the North Pole. The wolves there are white. They eat rabbits. They eat deer called caribou. The rabbits and caribou eat plants. They would eat all the plants without the wolves.

Wolves helped in North Carolina, too. Too many raccoons lived there. They ate most of the quail and turtles. Scientists brought back red wolves. The wolves eat raccoons. Soon there were more quail and turtles.

## Chasing Wolves

Smith checks on Yellowstone's wolves. But it can be hard to find them when they hide. So sometimes he uses a helicopter. A helicopter can chase a wolf that runs on the ground. Smith uses his dart gun. Bull's-eye! The dart hits the wolf. The wolf goes to sleep.

The helicopter lands. Smith jumps out. He checks the wolf's teeth. They are sharp. He weighs the wolf. It is a good checkup. The wolf is healthy.

Smith puts a special collar on the wolf. It sends a radio signal. It tells Smith where the wolf is. It helps him check on the wolf wherever it goes.

The number of wolves is growing in Yellowstone National Park. This makes Smith happy.

**Snow White.** *This Arctic wolf is white. It blends in with the snow.*

## Wolf Fear

Not everyone is happy about the wolf's return. What if wolves attack people? Many farmers and ranchers fear that wolves will eat their animals.

People are right to fear wolves. Wolves can be dangerous. They attack dogs and farm animals. In some places, wolves have attacked people.

Smith knows what to do. People can scare wolves away. They can make loud sounds. They can shine bright lights. Most wolves are afraid of people. They usually run away if people are near. Sometimes they hide because they fear people.

## Wordwise

**den:** a wolf's home

**endangered:** at risk of dying out

**pack:** a group of wolves

**reintroduction:** bringing back a plant or animal species to a place it once lived

# Join the PACK

Find out why wolves are making a big comeback. Then answer these questions.

**1** Describe two ways wolves send messages to each other.

**2** What happened to the number of wolves before 1973? What happened after 1973?

**3** How do wolves help plants and other animals?

**4** Where are wolves found in the U.S. today?

**5** How do people feel about bringing back wolves? Use both articles to answer.